# The Face Of Humanity

by

*Shirley Lanehart*

Copyright @ 2021 by **Shirley Lanehart**

All rights reserved. No part of this publication may be reproduced, distributed or transmitted in any form or by any means, without prior written permission.

Published by

**Positive Imaging, LLC**
Austin, Texas
http://positive-imaging.com
bill@positive-imaging.com

Photo Back Cover by **Marty Burnett**

**The Face Of Humanity/Shirley Lanehart**

**ISBN: 978-1-95177649-7**

# "LOVE PRECIOUS HUMANITY"

Harry Palmer

## Preface

The Soul is the link between the ground of being (our source) and our unique individuality. The Soul's language is prose and poetry. The Soul understands beauty, nature, poetry and music at a visceral level. It connects the above and the within encompassing the whole individual.

In this book, Shirley speaks the ineffable through poetry and prose. The Soul of each of us will recognize the truth that heals, connects us to all humanity and our Common Father. It relaxes the mind and opens the heart that one may see with new eyes. Shirley delivers the message that the Soul proclaims.

Barbara Cook
July 2021

# Introduction

Like the poems in *They Come to Teach*
these poems present themselves as universal in nature.
They are meant to be read slowly.
The meaning will be found in the pause after the reading more than in the words themselves.
It is my hope that *The Face of Humanity* will resonate with readers in a fashion that validates some part of their own inner journey and provide
an understanding that none of us are alone in our innermost thoughts and feelings.

Shirley Lanehart

True Humanity is within you

Seek and you will find it.

The Gospel of Mary Magdalene

(Gospel of Thomas, Matthew, Luke)

## *The Face of Humanity*

*I am the face of Humanity
Look in my eyes and see
The Glory of you and all mankind
From beginning to eternity*

*I am the face of Humanity
Feel my heart and know
I am in you and you are in me
We have the same place to go*

*I am the face of Humanity
Touch my body and hug my form
Another just like you
Living, breathing, moving
With many feelings too*

*I am the face of Humanity
Hear my message instead of my words
And you will know for sure
Humanity lives in you and me
And not an abstract world*

*I am the face of Humanity
A simple human being
You are the face of Humanity
Look in your eyes and see*

I Know Who I am

I Know What I am

I Know How I serve

Paul Selig

# Lamb Chops

Once upon a time there was a young girl whose name was Shirley. Shirley had a little lamb whose name was Lamb Chops. His fleece was white as snow. And everywhere that Shirley went the lamb was sure to go. And this is the rest of the story.

Shirley was born and raised in a large city. At age 13 her parents bought a ranch. Included in that purchase was a very smart Border Collie named Tip. All the sheep on the ranch were included in the purchase too. The family traveled back and forth from the city to the ranch on weekends and holidays.

One day they found an infant lamb whose mother had died. The lamb was brought to the house and bottle fed until it could eat solid food. The family gave him the name "Lamb Chops" and he knew his name well. Lamb Chops could be far away from the house but when his name was called he would come running just like Tip did when his name was called.  Lamb Chops traveled back and forth with the family from the city to the ranch just like Tip.

It came to be that although Lamb Chops knew his name and knew who he was he had forgotten what he was because Tip was like a mother to Lamb Chops.  Soon enough Lamb Chops began to behave a lot like Tip. However, Lamb Chop's behavior never got passed the puppy stage.  Lamb Chops would be so excited when he saw the family that he would jump up on their legs like a puppy would do.  He believed himself to be a dog and no one would ever convince him otherwise as long as he was part of the family.

That was all fun and well until Lamb Chops grew into a sheep. His hoofs, of course, grew with him. Those big hoofs began to hurt when he jumped on people in excitement to greet them.  He began to knock down Shirley's younger brother.  Lamb Chops was totally innocent in this hurtful and disruptive behavior. Lamb Chops had learned very well who he was but he had forgotten what he was.

One day when Shirley and her siblings came home from school Lamb Chops was missing. He could not be found anywhere.  It took a while for their father to summon the courage to tell the family what had really happened to Lamb Chops.  Everyone was imagining that Lamb Chops had somehow died.

Lamb Chops had not died. He had been taken to auction to be sold to another rancher. You can imagine the wailing that went on and the anger towards our father at doing such a cruel thing. Well our father was the wise one all along. Even though it was obvious that Lamb Chops was clearly a sheep the rest of the family had come to see him as a dog. Our father was the only one who had never forgotten that Lamb Chops was a sheep.

Our wise father allowed everyone to experience all their feelings of grief and loss. He even allowed the family's anger to be directed towards himself. Our father knew that no one could hear him until their initial reactions and hurt feelings had calmed down. When that happened he revealed his true intentions for taking Lamb Chops to auction.

Because Lamb Chops had learned who he was and would come when his name was called Lamb Chops had been sold as a lead sheep. This was very valuable to the ranchers. Flocks of sheep are not very smart. They are not good at protecting themselves and tend to scatter themselves and get lost easily. Sheep put themselves in danger by not staying together as one herd. This causes the rancher a lot of concern and time trying to find those stray lost sheep so he can protect them.

When Lamb Chops was joined with a flock of sheep he immediately remembered what he was and he looked like any other sheep in the field. But when his name was called at the end of the day (so the rancher could gather the sheep into a safe pen for the night) Lamb Chops would come running. All the other sheep followed Lamb Chops safely into the pen. He was a leader. Lamb Chops was an authentic and valuable lead sheep. Lamb Chops was a hero who helped the rancher protect all the sheep at night. Lamb Chops was never aware that he was hero. Perhaps it was good that Lamb Chops briefly forgot what he was and had learned who he was so he could become useful to the rancher.

Lamb Chop's story is not that much different than ours. We learn who we are through our family and culture and friends. What we are is often forgotten. Later, by realizing what we are, all of humanity becomes our family. It is then we are able to serve humanity without even knowing it. We hear the call from Our Common Father and because we have come to know who and what we are we respond with no thought of being a hero. We serve others simply by being who and what we always were from the beginning.

We are The Face of Humanity.

Try not to become a man of success,

but rather strive to become a man of value.

Albert Einstein

When you unify both halves of yourself,

You will become as you were originally created

Then if you say to the mountain,

"Move"

It will move.

The Gospel of Thomas
Matthew
Luke

## *Leap of Faith*

*Inside my mind lies a divided line
That no one else can see
One side is the truth of me
On the other a false reality*

*I lost my way somewhere in time
From the wisdom that made me free
Free to know the truth of me
Free to be all that I can be*

*I crossed that line long ago
And turned from truths that I know
I focused on values and judgments of others
I learned some lessons well
I wandered off my guided path
And made my own life hell*

*Chains of judgements, ideas and labels
Kept me in the dark
Until one day I came to see
The way to freedom in front of me*

*What I need, and I know this for sure,
Is a leap of faith through the door
Not to an unknown scary side
But across that line to where I hide*

*A giant leap from what I have learned
To the place where I came from
To a place that I already know
Where I crossed that line long ago*

In order to know everything you must

First know yourself

If you do not know yourself

Then, you know nothing

Those who know themselves also know the All

The Gospel of Thomas

## My Ego is my Friend

She didn't mean to do it
She thought it was best for me
Guided by illusions
She has kept me from being free

She has made me a fake
For my own good's sake
And I have watched her time and again

Who is this person who lives in me
Who gets in my face so that I cannot see
She has always been present and hard to handle.
She has taken a true life and made it a scandal

She's been with me for a very long time
And my thoughts on her were less than kind
We have been in a battle that no one could win
The only thing left was to try and be her friend

Yes maybe together
We can get through life
She can be the window
I can be the light

I can see the world
And the world can see me
She won't feel threatened
And I can be free

Life is from

The Inside Out

When you shift

On the inside

Life Shifts

On the outside


Kamal Ravikant

## *Bonita (Beauty)*

*And how are you within?*
*Is a frequent question*
*From my friend*

*It causes me to pause and then*
*Search much deeper from within*

*Honesty is crucial here*
*Within this seeing*
*Of which I fear*
*Dare I look inside*
*And see*
*A weeping willow*
*Inside of me*

*Oh what Beauty*
*I behold*
*When I abandon*
*What I have been told*

*I thank my friend*
*For the honest pause*
*To take a moment*
*To find the cause*

*The cause of this*
*Amazing moment*
*The inner knowing*
*Of pure atonement*

*What is here*
*I need not fear*
*Even if it is full of tears*

*And how are you within?*
*Is a frequent question*
*I ask my friends*

It is only with the heart that one can see rightly:
what is essential is invisible to the eye.


Antoine de Saint-Exupéry

## Connection

What an honor it is to know you
Out of all the people on earth
When I close my eyes and think of you
It is a privilege too moving for words

I see a person, a spirit, a friend
Whose presence has blessed me
Time and Again

I see you in light and love and peace
I hear the wisdom you have to teach

Drawn together by invisible hands
You show me the love that is in every man

For in your heart and in your soul
There is a treasure that is rich to behold

Except you become as children

You cannot enter

The kingdom of God

Jesus

## Lost in Play

Two children were playing
On a brisk fall day
They did not see me
They were lost in play

Time meant nothing
An hour slipped away
Absorbed in each moment
They were lost in play

Surrendering myself
I could remember a day
When thoughts were suspended
I was lost in play

To become as children
We each have a chance
To let go of ourselves
To get lost in the dance

And in that place
Where thoughts are let lay
Moving in spirit
We are lost in play

Two children were playing
On a brisk fall day
They did not see me
They were lost in play

All forms, all beings in the Universe exist

Within and in relationship to each other

In the end, all things will return

To their essential nature

The Gospel of Mary Magdalene

## Falling in Grace

Leaves are raining
As stillness waits
When the last one falls
She will have her way

And what is her way
But silent night
Bare limbs quiet
In the still moonlight

By day a grace
That is filled with faith
Waiting for spring
When she knows she will wake

In the meantime
It is letting go
One by One
Until she knows

Leaves are raining
So she can know
A silent night from long ago

Find a place of stillness

Within yourself

The Gospel of Thomas

# Lost in Copy

*Letter by Letter*
*The scribes of the past*
*Revealed the truth*
*So the Word would last*

*Printing presses soon came along*
*The presence of scribes*
*Became*
*Less Strong*

*Next came copy machines*
*The faster the better*
*Sheets of copy*
*Down to the letter*

*And now we have come*
*To cut and paste*
*We quickly cut*
*What we name waste*

*But what has been lost*
*In between*
*Is Authentic Truth*
*That can no longer be seen*

*Faster and Faster*
*We copy the past*
*And lose the present*
*The only thing that lasts*

*Lost in copy*
*Somewhere is Soul*
*What the scribes revealed*
*The Original Whole*

# Afterward

Most of these poems came to me within a 20 minute time frame. Unfortunately for me they woke me in the middle of the night. The basic frame (skeleton) was then hand written in the wee hours of the morning. After that came the days, sometimes months of editing to work on (as all poetry does) the impossible task of finding the perfect words to flesh them out. These poems became a sacred teacher for me throughout the years.

In his book *Faith after Doubt* Brian D. McLaren speaks of two different and equally important types of faith that can come to us at different stages in our life time.

Faith expressed as belief
And/or
Faith expressed as love

When I was 16 years old our minister asked the youth to teach the adult Sunday class perhaps as an experiment. The theme of my talk was simply that beliefs change like the weather but God's love, in which we trust, never changes.

More and more the faith that I have held through belief is giving way to a faith that can no longer be thought about nor spoken about in terms of belief.

The definition of faith expressed as belief makes great poetry, parables, metaphors, and mythology. There are times in our lives that these are vital to our faith.

In contrast there is no definition for faith expressed as love. It exists and expresses itself beyond words so there can be no misunderstandings or arguments. Nothing to fight a war about.

I am just now beginning to absorb the lessons from these poems and the talk I gave those many years ago. Silence is my sacred teacher now.

May Divine Love guide you wherever you are in your own amazing life journey.

www.ingramcontent.com/pod-product-compliance
Lightning Source LLC
Chambersburg PA
CBHW041220240426
43661CB00012B/1099